D0524673

T1.RMR.646

Hummingbirds are the tiniest of all birds

Hummingbirds

Jill Kalz

A⁺

Smart Apple Media

COPYRIGHT

Published by Smart Apple Media

1980 Lookout Drive, North Mankato, MN 56003

Designed by Rita Marshall

Printed in the United States of America

Photographs by KAC Productions (Kathy Adams Clark, Larry Ditto, Bill Draker, Greg W. Lasley), Root Resources (Anthony Mercieca)

Library of Congress Cataloging-in-Publication Data

Kalz, Jill. Hummingbirds / by Jill Kalz. p. cm. — (Birds)

Summary: An introduction to the physical characteristics, behavior, and life cycle of hummingbirds, the smallest birds in the world.

ISBN 1-58340-130-X

1. Hummingbirds—Juvenile literature. [1. Hummingbirds.] I. Title.

QL696.A558 K36 2002   598.7'64—dc21   2001049640

First Edition 9 8 7 6 5 4 3 2 1

CONTENTS

Small and Brave

It weighs no more than a penny. It can fly straight up, down, forward, and backward—even upside down! It seems to magically change color in the sunlight. And it is brave enough to attack creatures more than 100 times its own size! Meet the hummingbird. Hummingbirds are the world's smallest birds. They average three to five inches (8–13 cm) in length, but the tiniest, the bee hummingbird of Cuba, is just two inches (5 cm) long. More than 300 different kinds, or species, of hummingbirds live in South, Central, and North America.

Twenty-three species live in the United States and Canada, but

only the ruby-throated hummingbird can be found east of the

Rocky Mountains.

A male ruby-throated hummingbird

Hummingbird Details

Of all birds, hummingbirds are the best fliers. Their extremely strong chest muscles and specially designed wings allow them to move like helicopters. They can hover in mid-air, then zoom away in any direction, beating their wings an average of 50 times per second! The hummingbird's favorite food is **nectar**, but it also eats insects and tree sap. To feed on nectar, the hummingbird hovers in front of a flower blossom, then sticks its long bill inside. It laps the nectar with its tongue like a cat. Most hummingbirds have a tongue that is

twice as long as their bill. Plants help to feed
hummingbirds, but hummingbirds help plants too. Bits of
pollen collect on the birds' bills as they feed. As the birds

Hummingbird wings turn in any direction

Hummingbirds usually feed in mid-air

travel from blossom to blossom, the pollen falls off on different plants. The plants use the pollen to make seeds. Hummingbirds are often called "feathered jewels" because of their colorful **plumage**. Feathers can be just about any color, but what is most special is that they seem to change in the light. The ruby-throated hummingbird, for example, may look brown or black in the shade, but in the sun, its neck glows a bright red. This effect is called **iridescence**.

On an average day, the Rufous hummingbird visits up to 1,500 different flower blossoms.

In the light, hummingbird feathers shimmer

Building Tiny Families

When the weather turns cold, most hummingbirds **migrate**. These tiny fliers are strong enough to travel great distances. The ruby-throated hummingbird flies 500 miles (800 km) nonstop across the Gulf of Mexico. And the Rufous hummingbird flies all the way from Alaska to Central America!

 In the spring, the birds return and look for mates. Males try to attract females by putting on daring air shows. They dive from great heights, perform jerky "dances," and make loud, high-pitched calls. After mating, the male leaves, and the

female raises her young alone. She builds a nest in the fork of

a tree branch with grasses and bits of bark. Strands of spider

web hold the nest together. The finished nest is usually no

A hummingbird building a nest

bigger than a walnut. The female hummingbird lays two white eggs, each the size of a small jellybean. She sits on the eggs to keep them warm so the babies inside will grow. After about two weeks, the eggs hatch. Newly hatched hummingbirds do not have any feathers. Their eyes are closed. And they depend upon their mother to feed

Hummingbirds must eat every 10 minutes, all day long, to keep up their strength for flying.

them. With good care, though, baby hummingbirds are ready to leave the nest in just three weeks.

A mother hummingbird feeding her chick

Taking Care

The world can be a dangerous place for a tiny bird. Hawks can snatch a baby hummingbird from its nest. Long migrations often leave hummingbirds tired and sick. They may fly into window screens, spider webs, or thorns. Storms and sudden changes in temperature are **Some hummingbirds are so small that they can be captured by large insects such as the praying mantis.** also threats. Because of these dangers, the average life span of a hummingbird is just a few years. Although many hummingbirds are thriving, some hummingbird species are

endangered, especially in tropical areas. As human populations

grow, trees are cut down to make room for roads and cities.

Wildflowers are also destroyed. Without food and a place to

Hawks sometimes eat baby hummingbirds

build their nests, hummingbirds cannot survive.

Thankfully, many people are working to protect hummingbird **habitats**. Some people also hang feeders or plant special flowers to attract the birds. Whether we admire hummingbirds for their amazing flying abilities or for their colorful plumage, our love for these little birds will help to ensure their future.

Red and orange are hummingbirds' favorite colors; this is why most feeders are red.

A hummingbird feeder filled with syrup

Another Way to Fly

Unlike other birds, hummingbirds can take off straight up into the air, hover in one place, and dart in any direction. Because of this, hummingbirds are often compared to helicopters. This activity will show you how to make your own paper helicopter.

What You Need

A piece of typing paper
A pencil
Scissors
A paper clip

What You Do

1. Using the paper and pencil, trace the diagram on the opposite page.
2. Carefully cut along all solid lines.
3. Fold flap A toward you along the dotted line, and fold flap B away from you.
4. Fold flaps C and D toward the center. Flap D should overlap flap C.
5. Now, fold the bottom up along the dotted line. Secure it with the paper clip.
6. To make the helicopter fly, hold it over your head, paper clip toward the floor, and drop it.

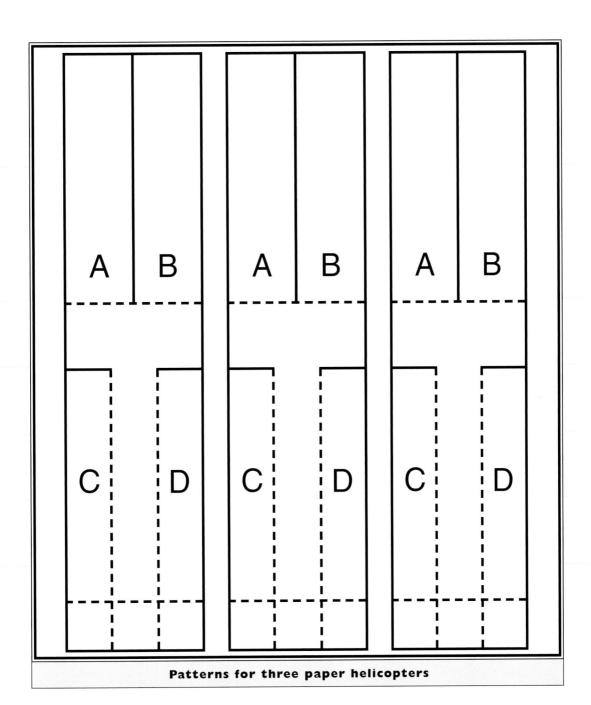

Patterns for three paper helicopters

23

Index

Words to Know

habitats (HAB-i-tats)—the areas where certain animals naturally live

iridescence (eer-eh-DEH-sents)—a shiny, rainbow display of color, like the colors on a soap bubble

migrate (MY-grate)—to move from one area to another according to the changing seasons

nectar (NECK-ter)—a sweet syrup produced by flowers

plumage (PLOO-mij)—a bird's feathers

Read More

Gerholdt, James E. *Ruby-Throated Hummingbirds*. Edina, Minn.: Abdo & Daughters, 1997.

Himmelman, John. *A Hummingbird's Life*. New York: Children's Press, 2000.

Stefoff, Rebecca. *Hummingbirds*. New York: Benchmark Books, 1997.

Internet Sites

About.com, Inc.: Birding/Wild Birds
http://birding.about.com/hobbies/
birding

Kid Info: Birds
http://www.kidinfo.com/science/
birds.html

The Hummingbird Web Site
http://www.portalproductions.com/h